About Hitchin
from my Prayer Journal
(1991 - 2014)

by

Bob Adams

Waysbrook Publishing

Copyright © Bob Adams 2015.
All rights reserved.

Unless otherwise stated, all Scripture quotes are taken from the King James version of the Bible (KJV).

Scripture quotations marked (NKJV) are taken from the New King James version of the Bible. Copyright © 1979, 1980, 1982 by Thomas Nelson Inc., publishers. Used by permission.

Scripture quotations marked (NIV) or New International Version are taken from the Holy Bible, New International Version. Copyright © 1973, 1978, 1984, International Bible Society. Used by permission.

Scripture quotations marked (YLT) or Young's Literal Translation are taken from The Young's Literal Translation Bible.

Scripture quotations marked (NLT) or New Living Translation are taken from the Holy Bible, New Living Translation, Copyright © 1996, 2004, 2007 by Tyndale House Foundation. Used by permission.

ISBN 978-0-9549269-4-6

Waysbrook Publishing

Preface

This is a collection of entries about Hitchin which have been taken from my own personal prayer journal. It has been compiled primarily for my own personal use and not for general publication.

For the most part, the events I have recorded in this book were written down shortly after they happened. I have set them down as I saw them or understood them. They are from my own perspective and according to my own grid of understanding at the time.

Should this book fall into the hands of others and evoke a response, feel free to contact me if you wish. I will endeavour to respond if I can.

Some of what I have written, other people may find difficult to understand. They may even find themselves in disagreement with me. I am not intending to be contentious or to offend. I am simply trying to record what has come to me or what I have seen. My heart is to get to know God more deeply. As far as it is in my power, I wish to come into alignment with what He is doing in me and through me, whether I fully understand it or not. So, I am not putting forward any new doctrine or theology, only experiences and thoughts, which at the end of the day may well be proved to be incomplete or even wrong.

Where I have spoken of other people, with exception of my wife Janis and others who are in the public eye, I have changed their names to protect their anonymity.

Lastly I acknowledge the wonderful love and trust of My Father God, who has such great faith in me. I acknowledge His patience and forbearance in allowing me to compile and print this book.

And if indeed anyone else reads this book, I would say to you, my unexpected reader, I bless you. I bless you in the name of Jesus, with a greater ability to allow the Holy Spirit of God to move in your life, to will and to do, that which is pleasing to Him.

So, do enjoy. I hope you will find something encouraging and edifying within these pages.

Bob Adams

CONTENTS

1	I give you Hitchin	1
2	St Ippolyts covered in young people	2
3	International Reconciliation Centre	3
4	I asked You what to believe for	3
5	Prophecy of Pastor Faith Agbor to Bob	4
6	Wells - another prophetic word from Pastor Faith	8
7	The Portal	13
8	The Portal again	13
9	The Portal - 3	15
10	The Portal - 4	15
11	The Portal - 5	18
12	The Portal - 6	20
13	In St Ippolyt's wood and sharing the vision	20
14	The Portal - 7 / IRC vision released	21
15	What does it mean to take a city	23
16	Joshua - a book of strategy	26
17	Taking the territory	28
18	Wells and worship	32
19	Lord I feel	33
20	Strategy Room in Heaven	36
21	From sitting in the Strategy Room	38

22	Proclamations	39
23	Declarations	41
24	More declarations	43
25	Meaning of Strategy & Tactics	44
26	Possible strategies of the enemy	45
27	God puts the lonely in families	46
28	IRC Prayer	46
29	IRC does not get the buildings	47
30	IRC strategy - 1	47
31	Possible IRC weekly timetable	48
32	Joshua again	49
33	Possible enemy strategy against revival	50
34	They belonged before they believed	50
35	A vision of Hitchin	51
36	This flowed off from above the Strategy Table	52
37	Stay in the classroom	52
38	I missed a call from Carolina	53
39	Some more about the Strategy Room	54
40	I had a brief time in the Strategy Room	55
41	It was at 4 pm	56
42	I give you authority over all the power	56
43	May I come into the Strategy Room	57
44	Check I have the answers	58

45	Everyone in the Strategy Room is waiting	59
46	My part in this	59
47	Authority over the land entails	63
48	Cafe Nero and seeing the seven Rs of the IRC	65
49	To Do - From previous journal entries	65
50	Prince of the power of the air Ephesians 2:2	68
51	In the Strategy Room	69

ABOUT HITCHIN
from my Prayer Journal

- - -

one day in August 1991

I give you Hitchin

I was standing in the kitchen in my house in Charlton, South East London, when out of the blue the Lord spoke audibly to me. He said, *"I give you Hitchin, young people first, then the older ones and the children."*

He showed me the young people on the seats in (what I thought was) the High Street (outside W H Smith) idling their time away.

He showed me a drug dealer near St Mary's church, at the top of the steps on the corner of the market, by the car park.

He showed me a cafe near the station, which had a Coca Cola sign outside, from where they ran teenage prostitutes.

- - -

Some time later I had the opportunity to travel to Hitchin with two of my sons and my mentor Pastor Donald Miller. We attended a Sunday morning service at the New Testament Church of God.

The last time I had been in Hitchin was in 1965, passing through, en route for France. I knew the big old church in the centre of town, but I did not know these other places as the town had changed a lot since 1965. However I saw them clearly in the vision.

I spoke to Pastor Rosetta, who pastored the New Testament Church of God in Hitchin. I told him about the vision.
After the morning church service he drove me round the town and those areas were exactly as I had seen them in the vision. I was very excited and expected to see God move then and there.

- - -

one day in August 1993

St Ippolyts covered in young people

I had been mowing the grass in the front garden of the house we rented on the London Road in St Ippolyts, which is a village about one mile south of Hitchin.

As I looked across the valley towards the church, suddenly the field across the road was covered in young people, all standing 6 feet apart from each other, in rows and columns - everyone quietly seeking the Lord.

The church had its lights on and was also involved. The lights in the school were on. That was also being used.

There were small groups strolling through the wood, chatting, using the wood for 'time-out'.

At the house and stables in the bottom of the dip as you go up to the church, there was a queue of people waiting for food and information about accommodation.

I just knew that young people were flooding here from all over

England and Europe, seeking the Lord, seeking reconciliation. A bit like Taizé.

- - -

29 December 1993

International Reconciliation Centre

I am still living in St Ippolyts. Coming out of the front door, the Lord suddenly bathed everything outside in a flash of blinding white light. He asked, *"Would you like St Ippolyts blitzed by the Lord, so that everyone is saved and is a minister of reconciliation?"*

I said, "But it is Hitchin I have been given as a burden, although I would not like to refuse, can you do the same for Hitchin?"

The Lord said, *"Don't you realize, St Ippolyts is part of Hitchin?"* Then I understood that Hitchin included the outlying villages too. And the Lord would give those as well.

I said, "Yes please, Lord."

He also gave me understanding that the International Reconciliation Centre (His words, not mine,) would be just a little way out of town, just as St Ippolyts is a little way outside Hitchin.

- - -

1 February 1995

I asked You what to believe for

I asked You Lord, to show me what to believe for, for the Hitchin revival.

I saw groups of two, three or four young people, bubbling with joy, running up to shoppers in Bancroft at the end of Hermitage Road.

I asked what are they doing?
They are sharing the gospel.

I saw Windmill Hill being used as a natural amphitheatre with a large group of people sitting on the grass listening to a speaker.

I saw crowds of young people flooding Bancroft Gardens wanting spontaneous worship meetings. Some had brought their guitars and were on the bandstand playing.

It was as if I were walking down West Hill. Each of the houses had lights on in their front rooms. Through the front windows, I could see families (and friends) having prayer gatherings.

So many happening all at once.

- - -

24 August 2012

Prophecy of Pastor Faith Agbor to Bob

(This prophecy was recorded and is transcribed below. Pastor Faith is from Nigeria and in some places his accent is difficult to decipher.)

You are deep. You dug a Well of Salvation before.
And (you) got out of that Well of Salvation. The enemy blocked some, because of disencouragement and weariness.

And this Well of Salvation is growing up again.
(This) well has been growing up, - growing up again.

And how I see it growing? It's growing up (in) like a place where there's like an oil spillage, - you know, - (and) no trees are allowed to grow in there.
When I see the type of this oil spillage, it turns to be fountains of water.
What the enemy thought they had used to have poisoned that which was in your hand, is coming now to work out the salvation in the life of many people.

Don't give up. Don't give up.
What He has spoken to you, about 5 years ago, in the night season, - now you were in tears when God was speaking to you, with a portion of the Scriptures, - He spoke to you in Isaiah.
Uh?
And you (were) meditating on it, and you were in tears, and the Glory of the Lord was all over you, asking God, when will the manifestation of this glory?. . when will be the manifestation of this glory? You were questioning God, the glory is more, the glory is more. You see, you fear(ed) God as He spoke to you from Isaiah.

And any time this word comes to you, Satan is going to contend with that word.
But listen. The stone which has been rejected by the builders is coming back to be the head corner of the house. And this will be the Lord's doing and it shall be marvellous in our sight.

OK?

The fountain of healing in you will not be covered.
?????????? has happened within the space of 5 years.
OK?

1. Your financial expectation was cut a little bit below.
2. Some friends you thought you have helped, have suddenly changed.
3. The work you thought you should be able to grow so fast, began to crumble.

God said, "It is my speed that I want you to follow. Not your speed."
He says, "I'm pruning you for ?another? purpose."

You (are) stepping in the world of Africa. Mmm?
There's a link between you and Africa. You get it?

And God is building on the anointing, not only for the environment, I suspect that He is going beyond the continent.

You are facing some battles now, but that battle is over. It's a terrible battle. Uh?
(It) threatens that and is targeting your marriage - Uh? - your marriage, your wife. Uh?
It will go.

But there is a link between you and Africa.
I don't know you before, but I see the flag of Africa in your life, some Africa(n) flags.

Pray more. Pray more.
You have more sons. You have more people. You have more people to raise in Africa.
When that is gone, the day, the gifts, of the charity organisation God has given to you will be over.
The gift to feed the hungry, heal the sick, raise the dead.

You are called by His name. Fear not. Amen.

There's some of your family members saying, "We told you ???? and you didn't hear us???? Like a mockery.
But the mockery will turn to miracles. Mmm?

It's like you are abandoned on that path of challenge, but in the midst of the abandonment there is an abundance of rain.

But erect the altar again. Put more fire on it.
And Elijah put the altar to shape first. Hmm?
And made the trench of the altar, and then he laid a sacrifice, and asked for water.
Water does not resemble that which will bring fire.

Until you are regenerated by the washing of the Word, there is no fire of the Holy Spirit.

I hear a word like 1957.
But I don't know how it's related to your life.
I don't know. OK?
I hear a word like 1957.
Listen.
Whatsoever friend has a link with your family name. Mmm?
1. Every time you are praying, say, "Lord, every spell of 1957, I reverse it." Mmm? "I reverse it." That is 1.
2. God is bringing you in contact with some of your family members for their total salvation.
Some of them will complain of some sickness.
Some of them will complain. . .
It is the anointing that God has given to you, that He will create a vacuum, where you will put that anointing, for them to believe

you or not.

But don't take it as brother (family relationship) when you go to them. Tell them I come in the name of the Lord.
If you go in the name of Brother, it will, nothing will happen.
If you go in the name Uncle, Brother, Sister, nothing will happen. When you go there, ingather in the name of the Lord, and you speak, God will take over that word to work on them. You will plant the seed, somebody will do the harvest.

- - -

31 August 2012

Wells
A word given by Pastor Faith Agbor specifically to me

There will have to be a depth of digging, you know, you are digging wells. It has levels. It has levels of digging. You will meet hard stones to crack, rocks to break.

A well is different from a cistern. A cistern holds less water and keeps it like a reservoir, whereas a well, you have to dig deep to hit the water underground, for it to come up.

So the water down is what serves the up. All the water that runs through the whole of London comes from the ground, whether it is a 100 storey building, it goes from down there. But the force with which it comes from the ground, determines the force with which it is going to move up. So, the deeper the better. The deeper the well, the fresher, the better it is. It's the most secure, the most protected.

So ?real? waters are not gotten from the shallow face. You have

to dig a little bit.
It's going to take training, retraining, and re-soaking.
Then, by the time you are out of it, because God is going to give you a combination of two things – the Word and the Spirit; the combination of both, to run with what He has given to you.

So those are the things.

So, then I ?saw? that unless a seed of corn falls to the ground and dies, it abideth alone.
So there's going to be a level of one release – you release yourself and allow some of that process, for you to really go through - and dig to deeper, a little deeper, a little deeper. Then after that you will be able to ?reach? some with real ministry, that God will be able to release you to a level.
But there's going to be, after [a] (that) release, [there's been a release,] then there's going to be another release.
So, release (number) 1 (is going to be a) release by the Spirit of God.
(Then) there's coming (a) release by the apostolic, by training.
Then (there is coming) a release by hitting the fountain, a supernatural one.

So, one is natural - leading to the call.
One is by training.
The other one, (the third one) is the supernatural, which you will be able to discover by yourself.

Then you grow there, because ministry, of what it is, is not what you are told. It is going to be what you are - encountered by God.

So while you hit and dig the well, your hands will peel, you sweat over it.

Well diggers don't wear suits to dig wells.
In Africa, you can still know that farmers don't wear ????, but when the harvest comes, the joy goes everywhere in the world.

So those are the things.
That is where God is just . . .
It's going to be very deep, very deep.
And God is going to really get . . . many things are going to be released now, to you, that you are still going to ?preserve? and cook in prayer.
The more you cook it, the stronger you will become.

So there is a release coming, a supernatural (one) coming.
The training has gone forth.
The natural, a substance of what God has called you to do is there.
(So) remain in the supernatural.

It is not going to be a system. It's going to be a spirit.
It is not going to be an organisation. It's going to be an organism.
Organisation is man made. Organism is God made, is divine.

[And when people come and contend for your well?]
You have to fight for your well.
Yes, that's Genesis 26.

You have to dig. Let's say he digged - Abraham.
They covered it.
The prophetic covering of that well, is that God was true with Abraham.

He digged another one. They covered it.
Although he reopened it, that was a dealing with the circumcision, the covenant of circumcision he had.

Now God wanted to have a personal encounter. That is called Rehoboth.
Your Rehoboth cannot be covered.
It will invite your friends and your enemies to come and drink from the same well.
But the Father of . . . that of Abraham, you can't explain how it came, he only try and maintain a covenant.

He gets and digs another one.
He was only trying to maintain a covenant; a covenant of circumcision and rest. That is it.
God said 'No, it must be covered. Do you redig what I want in personal contact. Then he dug again. He make a Rehoboth.

So the digging of the well, that's what I am saying, - 3 times –
the natural realm,
the supernatural realm,
and the training.

The training is just you have yielded yourself - that's a cost and you have done well. Then that training is going on. You are going to hit the Rehoboth – I'm saying Abraham's well.

He opened another one and called it Esek. (strife)
He opened another one, different names he called it.
But that was not what God was after. God was after Rehoboth and not a ?second? rest.
And then they couldn't contend with him over it.

So there are going to be contentions in training,
and understand you are going to be misunderstood
and abused,
but it doesn't matter.

Just keep maintaining the flow.
That is, you redig and maintain the flow.
You don't close down the flow.
Because you will still need those wells to support your Rehoboth. ?Case you are ???? to have a problem, so have 2 wells to support your Rehoboth. You are not going to shut it down and say, 'OK, maybe I go to my Rehoboth, until my Rehoboth comes.' You need those 2 wells to keep drinking until your Rehoboth comes.

So you have to redig.
Don't go backwards.

So, a little patience. You are going to hit it and hit it well.

Now you are running together with a level and that some times you are going to run alone into that Rehoboth and then the whole world will get ?of? it.

OK?

So those are the things.

So it is going to involved some itinerary.
I mean there's going to want some outreaches, left and right.

But there is going be a submission to the ministry as your pastorate.
There's going to be something like a school that will run as, you are going to have a pastor, which is what God is trying to do for you, so you that have somebody as you say you have as your pastor, so you can be free with. He knows you. You know him. These are the things I'm doing, until you give me time to prayer about it.
That patience is to give you a muzzle.

So you say, my pastor is praying about it. I am praying about it. You join us in prayers, that's all.

And by the time you meet God, He will speak the same thing. So backing of those things, it's going to be supernatural.

- - -

25 May 2013

The Portal

Took Janis out to town.
Took mum's watch to Glenray's to be repaired.
Dropped into Foxholes and took in the vase and tights to mum.

On talking to Janis, I explained that the portal, (which felt a bit like an open heaven,) which Jonathan and I felt near Hexton, the other side of the road to the manor, had moved.

The last time I went to Deacon's Hill to have time-out with God, I had passed through it when previously it was almost on top of Hexton. It was now by Tingley House.

So we drove down the Pirton Road so I could show Janis.

It was now past Tingley House, and has moved towards Hitchin.

- - -

19 July 2013

The Portal again

Anthia went to experience the portal for herself.
It had now come to just inside the town limits - just past Foxholes,

and centred over High Point.

She sent me this text at 18:20 -
*A conversation I think I had with the Lord at High Point, Hitchin.
It started by a sense I was hearing distant cries / clamour.
I asked Father, "What are You doing here?"
"Visiting my people! I have heard their cries."*

*I asked, "What do we have to do?"
The question came - When a visitor comes. . . , what do you do?*

*I answered, "I open the door to them and invite them in."
"I am knocking at the door of their hearts."*

*I asked, "How can we help?"
"Tell my people I love them. I want to come in and eat with them."*

*I asked, "What can we do?"
"Pray. Thy kingdom come. Thy will be done.
Thy kingdom come. Thy will be done.
Thy kingdom come. Thy will be done.
I have sent you as a prophet to the nations. . .
Start with Hitchin.
Proclaim that the day of the Lord's favour is at hand.
All who turn and seek His face will find rest for their souls.
For in My presence there is fullness of joy.
Go.
Tell my people
I am coming
I am here."*

*(I answered) "What if they won't listen?"
"That's not for you. You are the mouth ... you and all Bob's people.*

Start with your churches.
Start with your pastors.
Start!"

"What if we don't start?"
"A darkness will come. A great darkness will cover My people.
This is the time of the visitation of the Lord.
Rise, shine, for the light has come
And the glory of the Lord is risen on you."

My response was, "Please help us, Lord. Open up the heavens, pour out a blessing.
Lord we need refreshing till it overflows..
Rain, rain on me.
Open up the windows of heaven. Amen.

(At this point my phone overheated and shut down.)

- - -

25 July 2013

The Portal - 3

Rowena reported that she had felt the Presence as she was driving through to Luton on the A505.
She was sure it had moved again and was in one of the side roads past where she drove.

- - -

26 July 2013

The Portal - 4

I went to see Pastor Angus in Luton this morning. As I was

leaving Hitchin on the A505 (Offley Road/Moormead Close - still within the town), I sensed the presence of the portal, just as Rowena had said.

On returning to Hitchin from my visit to Luton, I turned into Carter's Lane just before I came into the town, in order that I could approach Hitchin on the Pirton Road (B566).
I drove back into Hitchin past Foxholes and past High Point, but the portal wasn't there.

I continued down the hill to the mini roundabout, where it joins the A505, the road from Luton, and I started to sense the presence again.

I turned back on the A505 towards Luton as if I wanted to leave Hitchin again and travelled up Offley Road and this time turned into Moormead Close. Although I was near, it wasn't there.

I turned round and rejoined the A505 toward Luton. At the bottom of the hill as you leave Hitchin, I turned left into Willow Lane. Wow! The portal was half way along.
The traffic was busy. I drove to the end of the road and turned left onto the Ring Road, back to the roundabout at the library and then again started on the A505. This time I navigated toward Minsden Nursing Home, trying to run parallel to Willow Lane. I took Meadow Way and then into Cranbourne Avenue. I parked up in one of the little slip roads off Willow Lane and started talking to the Lord.

(Interestingly the portal has changed direction and seems to be skirting Hitchin, heading toward Charlton and maybe Gosmore and possibly St Ippolyts.)

It felt like I was in the presence of the Lord's angel. The conversation I had went like this:

What are you doing here, lord?
"I am in transit."

Are you for Hitchin?
"I am for everyone." (I had the sense of nations.)

Are you happy, lord?
"I have great anticipation."
(And then it is as though the Lord Himself is speaking.)
"I have great faith that my people will hear and respond."

What do we have to do?
"Pray, 'Thy kingdom come. Thy will be done on earth as it is in heaven.'"

Lord, what do we have to do to prepare for it strategically?
"Know your places - where you will be used.
Be content with your roles."
(I had a thought flash through my mind of the seven deacons who were elected in Acts. They served willingly. They were content to serve.)
"Know your places of ministration (serving).*"*
Keep your eyes on Jesus and keep doing what you have been appointed to do.
There is lots more happening than you can see, than you know.
You are part of the plan.
This is the hour, this is the time you have been made for.
You are all that you need to be at this moment.
The plan is not your plan. It is Mine, being done as I please, in the way that I wish and in My time.

Yes, you can miss it if you do not respond, if you do not wish to be available.
Hold yourself to be available."

Lord, I do not wish any should perish but that all should come to eternal life.
"I want that also, much more than you do."

I praise You Lord God, and I bless You.

- - -

30 July 2013

The Portal - 5

I went to check on what I have been calling the 'portal'.

I drove back to Willow Lane, entering it from the Ring Road and immediately sensed the Presence.

I turned left into Charlton Road, pulled onto the side of the road and parked. I just sat there allowing the quite heavy drops of sparkly spiritual rain to touch me. It was so nice to sit in that presence.

(What I had omitted from my entry of 26th was having a sense of there being a large angel standing there. On that day, after I had come out of Carter's Lane and was driving into Hitchin on the Pirton Road, something impressed itself on me and it came out of nowhere. I had a sense that the angel was about 4 or 5 houses tall, standing just over the hill, where High Point was, just inside the perimeter of Hitchin. I didn't see him. I could almost see him, but I couldn't see him. I had a strong sense of him being there - it was not a 'Bob imagination', it was a very strong impression that I knew he was there. I looked to see him there, I could almost see him, but I couldn't - if that makes any sense.)

Anyway, back to now.
I parked up at the start of Charlton Road and asked the Lord.
"What is it Lord?" (Meaning, what are You up to Lord?)
I received the answer that he was an installation angel.
OK... So he is bringing something to install.
(I wondered if it was an open heaven portal - somehow I still have this portal thing on my mind.)

I then clearly felt the prompting of the Lord that I should drive further down the road, and I would discover something more. So I drove on.

I arrived at the Windmill Pub and parked in the car park facing the fields.
Wow. The presence was stronger there than where I had parked before.

I just knew that the angel was old and often used before by the Lord. His assignment was not particularly big in Heaven's scale of things, but he is pleased to serve the Lord and His creation.

I know he is in transit and going to install something
(which I hope will be a permanent fixture for this town),
but I wondered if he had a series of installations to do and not just one.
(Now this is speculation on my part, but I reasoned why not? Suppose he installed several 'open-heaven portals' as part of God's end time plan. Wishful thinking maybe.)

After a while of just sitting in that presence I felt as if it was time to go and so continued driving up the road through Charlton. And then I got lost, ending up in the village of Preston.

According to the map, if the angel continues on his present course he will arrive in Gosmore next.

It was such a drizzly day, but I felt so refreshed and vibrant.

- - -

2 August 2013

The Portal - 6

I went back to Charlton to check on the angel, but he was no longer there.
I suspect he continued in his direction and has gone across the fields where I can't drive.

- - -

9 August 2013

In St Ippolyt's wood and sharing the vision

I went to spend time with the Lord at St Ippolyt's wood.

As I was on my way, I saw a notice on one of the field gates in the valley by the forge about discussions of using various fields for housing as part of the development expansion of West Stevenage.

I took it to prayer and continued to park behind the church. I walked through the graveyard to the wood. To my surprise the wood had been fenced in with new fencing.

I felt the prompting of the Lord to return to the church. As I walked the path to the little church an elderly man came in the opposite direction. He greeted me.

(Remembering that blessings come in different shapes and sizes and packagings,) I asked him about the fencing in and the signs.

He said that the locals were annoyed at the fencing in. The land had been bought by a new owner. (There were now steers on it.) He also allayed my fears and said it is unlikely planning will be given for the land to be used for housing - although the owner of the small field at the bottom of the dip opposite the forge has made it known that he would welcome being bought out by developers.

I shared with the man that I had previously lived in St Ippolyts and also the vision the Lord had given me of young people all over the upper field. (I wondered, 'Why was I doing this?')

I spent some quiet time in the church and returned to the upper field which I had seen in the vision years before. On impulse I stopped the car and started to prayer walk the field.
'Everywhere you put your foot, I will give you,' was running through my mind. I walked diagonally across the field claiming it in the name of Jesus.

- - -

9 August 2013

The Portal - 7 / IRC vision released

Having left the wood and field in St Ippolyts, I returned to the car in order to return home, but first I was going to find where the angel/portal was.

On the way to the car, the Lord started talking to me about prophets releasing the vision.

We already know that until the Word is spoken, the Lord does not do it. This is why He *does nothing without revealing it to His servants the prophets, first.*
Now I understand why the Lord uses His servants the prophets. Man has to speak it into being. Man has to agree for the Lord to do it (give permission - because of freedom of choice).

I drove into Gosmore cutting through the back roads. There was a shimmering. I was on the edge of it.

I was prompted to turn right down Mill Lane and then right again down Mill Road. (I had to turn round at one point and go back, because I drove past. I had not held myself sufficiently in readiness to the prompting of the Lord.)

To my surprise I came into The Crescent, where I had previously lived.
I turned left towards the London Road and paused at the corner. The shimmering was still there.
I knew it was not in the field on the other side of the road.
So I turned left towards Hitchin, expecting to have to turn left towards Gosmore again.

I was surprised again because the Presence was just a little way up the road towards Hitchin. On its journey, it had almost reached St Ippolyts.

I drove up the road through the area of the Presence, releasing the vision to come to pass in this place and asking the angel if he knew where to go. He did.

In Jesus' name, I release the vision of the Centre of Reconciliation into that place, into that atmosphere. I give permission for the Lord to bring it into being - that place where thousands will come to find reconciliation.

I had the sense that the vision had been born.
It was there.
It was done.
It will happen now.
Hallelujah!

- - -

30 March 2014

What does it mean to take a city

Lord, what does it mean to take a city?
In the natural you would conquer it.
In the spiritual you would conquer it.

Does it mean that you get everyone saved?
I have given man free choice to choose Me or not choose Me, so the answer is No.
I have exalted My Word above My Name. But it does mean that you overcome the spiritual atmosphere so that a situation like in Daniel 10 does not happen. For those who know Me, there is an open heaven and an ease of access without angelic/demonic interference.

Even though there are mosques and temples in the town?
Overcoming and walking in your authority will not mean that

people will necessarily stop worshipping their false gods, but the consequences are very different since the spirit realm is under your authority - and you are to exercise your authority.
Look back at what Jesus did. The demons just called out at Him. They had to. They had no back up. They had no support. Jesus took dominion of the spirit realm in all the places he went. The demons were isolated and coming face to face with the Presence of God in Jesus.
In Nazareth, it was the people who had lack of faith, not the demons or the spirit realm or the sickness or the madness. But a hard-hearted people that will stop you working, because I require that the free choice and wishes of each person is respected.

Is the Presence the same as the Anointing?
The anointing is a gift. People walk in the anointing even after they have made some errors and have walked away (from Me) *and are walking in a different path. Don't take the anointing as a certificate of approval from God. The only way you judge a tree is by its fruit. The anointing is a gift which is given. It is not a measure of character. Indeed the greater the anointing, the greater the depth of character needed to husband it. Like all gifts, the anointing can be stirred up in those people to whom it has been given and they can still use it, even though they may have chosen to walk another path. But the gift of anointing (and here I am not talking about the Holy Spirit as in John 3) will not keep that person on the straight and narrow* (but will lead). *They have to make continual choices to do that.*
In 1 John, the Holy Spirit is referred to as the Anointing which abides within, and who will teach you all things and lead you in all truth.

The Presence is different. It comes from unity. See Psalm 133. And the Presence can only flow when you are in harmony with Father. Here you see the Presence referred to symbolically as anointing oil. But the Presence of God will only be on one who is in alignment and unity with Father.

To walk daily in the Presence of God, is to walk daily in alignment with His will and His wishes.
This type of obedience only comes from a surrendered life of a dead person, where nothing anyone says or does, moves him, or intimidates him, or makes him change his stance.

Lord, how do I take a city?
Who are you? What authority do you have? Who do you have with you, who understands how the spirit realm operates? Have they not been assigned to minister to you who are the heirs of the Kingdom?

But what about the ungodly who lend their faith to the enemy to bring into being that which should not be?
The enemy forces have been vanquished and stripped. They have been spoiled. That means their armour and their weapons have been taken from them. They no longer have authority. I said that all authority and power had been given unto Me and told you to go into all the world and make disciples of all nations. You cannot make disciples of people who have not chosen Me or who have not given over their lordship to My lordship.
So in your city there will be disciples, and also self-centred and self-determining people, who do their own things and go their own way. They are not ready to submit their lives to the lordship of Christ.
But you do not have to suffer having a ruling spirit of darkness

over the land, blocking, hindering and broadcasting their messages to the demons - only if you choose to have them there or choose not to do anything about them.

Do you remember what I said when you asked Me to protect and hide you when reading that SRA information. I told you to, Arise and shine for your light has come, and the glory of the Lord is risen upon you.

Now put that into its context - for gross darkness has covered the people - that is why you are to arise and shine. So where there is darkness, you are to be light. That is not an option. It is a part of My plan of salvation in which you can co-operate. A disciple who does not walk in his authority is not bringing light to the people. You cannot be a person who learnt My disciplines and not do the same things as I did when on earth. The very deed of healing and deliverance shows forth the glory of God and the glory of God is risen upon you, so you must arise.

- - -

8 April 2014

Joshua - a book of strategy

Lord, You brought me back to Joshua, again.

Many years ago, when we first moved to Hitchin, and I used to commute daily by train to my work in London, I used to read my Bible on the train. I had been praying for Hitchin and when I came to the Book of Joshua, You told me to reread it and reread it and reread it. You told me then, that in that book (of Joshua) was the plan to take Hitchin.

At that time I was tired and stressed with the family situation and got bored with rereading Joshua and then drifted into doing other things in my Bible reading time.

That was about 20 years ago. And I know it was the strategy for taking Hitchin. And whilst in my head I thought it was a good idea, my heart wasn't in it, because I had too much on my plate - so to speak - fresh from the family break up, and still ouching from my unhealed brokenness.

And now You bring me back there.
Yes, I do Robert.

But this time it is different. Over the years I have matured somewhat, and received a great deal of healing. My self-worth has been restored and I am beginning to learn discipline in relation to You and the protocol of how You do things.

I am also understanding more of what You have placed on me, and who I am, in terms of privilege, to share in the rollout of Your plan.

After the March 2014 PDS-UK Conference at Our Lady's Church in Hitchin, I had a phone call about the collapsing of the Hitchin satanist coven. They had planned a sacrifice for the same time as when our conference was happening. For some reason they saw us as a threat.

At the point when the baby was about to be murdered as the sacrifice, something happened between the 13 adult coven members. (There were children there also.) The adults fell out with each other and started fighting among themselves. Three of them were floored. The person with the knife told the mother to take the child and get out. He/She then turned the knife on him/herself, such that he/she had to be hospitalised.

I was told that out of it, three of the members received Christ as their Lord and Saviour. The mother also asked how she could get out of satanism. She was told that the only way out was Jesus. She was also told to register the baby, straight away.

I asked You how all this came about, and how we had such effect? How come we have that level of authority in the land? You reminded me of the time, while we still lived in London, when You said, 'I give you Hitchin.'
You also reminded me of the prophecy of Isabel Allum, in which I was told that 'the Lord will give you authority over the land.'

I was sharing this with Angus. He immediately asked, "So, what is your strategy for taking Hitchin?"

I didn't have one. I hadn't even thought about it.
Then, in my Bible reading, You bring me back to Joshua - again. It is already there and You had already told me, 20 years before! But I wasn't ready to hear it.

Now I need to unpack it.

- - -

8 April 2014

Taking the territory

Last Friday, I spent until lunchtime, quiet before You in the chapel at Christchurch. I was thinking of strategy - strategy for taking Hitchin. I was thinking about how You directed Joshua.

Clearly You are not expecting me to physically exterminate all the human population with the edge of the sword, as Joshua did at Jericho and throughout the Promised Land.

And since the Old Testament is a shadow of things revealed in the New, I assume You expect, and it must be possible, to clear the land (Hitchin) of all spirits of darkness that have been assigned and residing in the town, leaving people's freedoms free from demonic interference.

Jesus, You laid waste all the Principalities, Powers and all Satan's kingdom, when You died at Calvary and descended to the dead.
Death could not hold You.
There was no spiritual legal right for the wages of sin to hold You.

And because of the illegitimate killing You suffered, Satan had to forfeit everything he had. The price You paid on Calvary was not only man-size, but it was also God-size. You were the Lamb of God who takes away the sin of the world.

Jesus, You said, "All authority has been given to Me."
And "I give you authority over all the power of the enemy."

And then You ascended to the Father where Satan could not touch You ever again, because he had been banished from heaven.

Jesus, You have the keys of Hades and Death.
A person with keys determines who goes in and who goes out. They can unlock the door/gate or lock up the door/gate. Jesus, You are the gatekeeper.

So how do we exterminate the spiritual mafia controlling Hitchin? How do we extract the spirits and what do we do with them?

We have been given the command to administrate the Kingdom of God here on earth. How can we do that with all the enemy

forces/agents running all over the place, interfering and causing havoc?
We do not allow this in ministry, so why do we allow it in general life?

Do we just put them into prison?
Do we dispose of them to a more permanent place of safe keeping?
Is there a more permanent place of safe keeping?

- - -

Revelation 1:18
I *am* he that liveth, and was dead; and, behold, I am alive for evermore, Amen; and have the keys of hell [*Hades*] and of death.

Revelation 20:1
And I saw an angel come down from heaven, having the key to the bottomless pit [*abussos - abyss, deep, (bottomless) pit*] and a great chain in his hand.

Revelation 20:3
And cast him into the bottomless pit [*abussos - abyss, deep, (bottomless) pit*], and shut him up, and set a seal on him, that he should deceive the nations no more, till the thousand years should be finished: and after that he must be released a little season.

Luke 8:28
When he saw Jesus, he cried out, and fell down before Him, and with a loud voice said, "What have I to do with Thee, Jesus, *thou Son of God Most High? I beseech Thee, torment me not!*"

Luke 8:31
And they besought Him that He would not command them to go out into the deep [*abussos - abyss, deep, (bottomless) pit*].

Revelation 9:1-2

And the fifth angel sounded, and I saw a star fall from heaven unto the earth: and to him was given the key to the bottomless [*abussos - deep, (bottomless) pit*] pit (*phrear - hole, well, pit*).

And he opened the bottomless [*abussos - abyss, deep, (bottomless) pit*] pit (*phrear - hole, well, pit*), and there arose smoke out of the pit (*phrear - hole, well, pit*) as the smoke of a great furnace; and the sun and the air were darkened by reason of the smoke of the pit (*phrear - hole, well, pit*).

Revelation 9:11

And they had a king over them *which is* the angel of the bottomless pit [*abussos - abyss, deep, (bottomless) pit*], whose name in the Hebrew tongue *is* Abaddon, but in the Greek tongue hath *his* name Apollyon.

Revelation 11:7

And when they shall have finished their testimony, the beast that ascendeth out of the bottomless pit [*abussos - abyss, deep, (bottomless) pit*] shall make war against them, and shall overcome them, and kill them.

Revelation 17:8

The beast that thou sawest was, and is not; and shall ascend out of the bottomless pit [*abussos - abyss, deep, (bottomless) pit*] and go into perdition: and they that dwell on the earth shall wonder, whose names were not written in the Book of Life from the foundation of the world, when they behold the beast that was, and is not, and yet is.

- - -

16 April 2014

Wells and worship

How to dig a well/portal

When we used to drive into Sunderland, in the days when the House of Prayer was operating on a 24/7 basis, there was a point between Washington and Sunderland, as you approached the town, when you penetrated what felt like an invisible force-field shield. I would start tingling all over, because of the presence of God in the place.

It wasn't that the drivers were any more courteous on the road, or that businesses were any less after our money, or the local youth were any the more accountable to their parents or society, but one knew that there was an open heaven in that place.

I remember, at the Revival Alliance Conference in 2012, during one of the breaks, I asked Pastor Faith Agbor to explain his preaching on wells. I hadn't understood all of it because of his Nigerian accent.

It had to do with aquifers.

Wells of the Kingdom are upside down.
They reach from earth to heaven.
They are dug by praise and worship.
They produce an open heaven.
They are portals.
It is our decision whether or not to engage with the Kingdom in this way.

We can allow the spiritual clouds of darkness to keep us in an overcast situation through doing nothing.

Yes the clouds are pushed back through praise and worship. And intimacy is easier on a fine day with the Sun of Righteousness rising with healing in His wings (zitzits).
It is easier to engage in that type of environment, when God makes a person wait on Him.
It is because God is wanting us to wait on Him (being pro-active), rather than it being (reactive) because of a hindrance from the enemy (Daniel 10).

(I will have to continue this later, because I am being called away.)

- - -

(*My part in this*)

- Waiting on the Lord and worshipping Him is key.
- Wells - access to the River of Life - is dug through worship. An open heaven is maintained through worship
- The army went out to battle carrying the Presence of God with them on the shoulders of the Levites.
- We are temples of the Presence. We must want and ensure God is able to abide in us.
- We are to be proactive in involving Him. We must watch and listen to His direction.
- We are not to presume His will is the same as what we think He should be doing. Check.

- - -

18 April 2014

Lord I feel

Lord, I feel, I have the witness, that another onslaught of sickness is trying to gain entrance into the family. This has been consistent in that every few days, sometimes every day, I sense the attack coming.

And as I write this, Holy Spirit, You acknowledge this.

I have a strange sense that there is a concerted attack as though demons are being sent, carrying sickness, carrying contention, carrying strife, carrying unwise decisions, carrying diversions to hinder family unity.

I wonder if the reports I have received that satanists are fasting and praying against Angus and me are true. I wonder, who are we that we should be so important?

Robert, I have called you. I have anointed you. I have the task for you to do. I have given you authority over the land. I have given you the mantle of father, leader, teacher, encourager, conqueror and son.

You are in My love. This is not as the culture of the world. In Me is not Yes and No, but Yes and Amen.

It is already settled in My heart. I am not having second thoughts about what I am wanting of You. I made My mind up ages ago, before the foundation of the world - you know this. This vacillating has to stop.

Just the same way you plunged yourself into Me, trusting Me, trusting Me with your eternal salvation, trusting Me to be your God - so too, plunge yourself into who you are, what I have made you to be.

It is not because of any merit of your own. It is because I made you and have ordained you to be what you are. It's just that your thinking, which you prize so much, hasn't caught up with it. It needs proof. It wants confirmation over and over, because these things are connected to some bad education, bad instruction about humility and pride, which have blocked you from embracing the truth, when it doesn't fit with what you think you should be in servanthood and humility.

Your vision is skewed. It is not seeing right. What you are seeing is not what I have ordained or wished for your life.

It is true that you are not all those things that I have called you to be. You will grow more and more in them. But don't worry about it. I am the craftsman and not you. It is my responsibility to make your frame into whatever I wish, for whatever purpose I choose to make you.

So.

It is not pride to recognise the apostolic calling on your life.

It is not pride or big headedness to recognise that you have a role of importance in the land for this time.

It is false humility to deprecate yourself.

It may not be socially acceptable, but then the world is under the sway of the evil one.

You have rarely been socially acceptable during your life.

Yes, being an apostle comes with the responsibilities of the job. Worldly Christians look at the title as if it were some kind of pedestal to receive praise and privileges from other Christian folk. But it is a job with responsibilities.

And remember, to whom much is given, much is expected.

Being a father, being in authority, being a leader, being a teacher are all jobs that may be difficult at times and have grave responsibilities. You need Me in all of that.

In My word from Isabel Allum, you are called a friend of God. You wanted that a long time ago. You asked me that a long time ago. Yes. I want you as friend also. I want to be able to share with you and you share with me.

I know your blocks and closets and hiding places. I know where you are at and what is happening with Janis. I told you just to thank Me for her healing. Continue doing that. Don't be deceived by what the eyes tell you.
My ways are not your ways. You cannot second guess what I am going to do, how I'm going to do it or why I am doing it. That is not your job. And don't try to rationalise everything.

Walk with Me. And let Me walk with you. You are here for a purpose.
Remember back to 27th April 1986. You were on your way home from church, after Holy Spirit fell as fire on you. I said to you, I give you a scripture for your life. And you didn't know your Bible then. You went home and looked it up and were astounded. Do you remember the time when I spoke to you and said that you were born for the great end-time revival. You didn't know what that meant. That language wasn't used in those days.

Let Me work out my purposes and enjoy the ride. My thoughts towards you are for good and not for evil, so quieten yourself as a weaned child on the breast of its mother. And allow Me to be your God and not your servant.

- - -

27 April 2014

Strategy Room in Heaven

Whilst at LGCC, the Lord was showing me that whilst there is a Strategy Room in heaven, so too should this be copied on earth.

We are to be so in tune with what is decided in heaven, that it should be implemented on earth - and that means seeing heaven's strategy for our churches, our businesses, our families as well as our personal lives. We should be so in tune that our personal lives reflect the strategies of heaven.

Proclamation, declaration, decreeing a thing are most important, and like strategies, we should research them and put them into practice.

If we declare Jesus as saviour and not deliverer, people will get saved but not delivered. Jesus said that the word preached will be confirmed by signs and wonders.

If our declarations or proclamations are not full-gospel, the results will not be full-gospel, even if our expectation might be for the Lord to do everything. But if we preach a full gospel, then the Lord is free to confirm our gospel with signs following.

The other thing which the Lord let me see was that apostles are as necessary to the Body of Christ as the local churches. We should push through the mindsets which divides the Body of Christ in our towns.

The local churches need the authority of the apostle, as well as the ministry of the seers. They need the authority of the person who is over the town, else they are going nowhere.

We have to disperse the lies that each individual church or denomination is an independent, autonomous unit. It may be organisationally in the physical, but in the spirit realm it is not.

- - -

19 May 2014

From sitting in the Strategy Room

Develop the habit of making proclamations.
Declare a thing and it shall come to pass.
Decree a thing and it shall be established.
Proclamation must be something we do in our prayer time, in our church time and in our business time. It is not optional.

Be a light which shows up compromise and absurdity.
Push through mindsets which divide the Body of Christ in our town. They need the authority of those who oversee the town.

Pray for the circumstances of the town.
Disperse the cloud of lies that each church is an independent autonomous unit.
Daniel prayed 21 days. No one came to help Gabriel, except Michael one of the chief princes. We are to stand together.

The strategy room protocol is to be copied on earth as it is in heaven.
It is to be in our personal spiritual life, our personal family life, our corporate church life, and our business/marketplace life.

Protocol:
    Sit with the light.
    Be light around the table.
    Let the strategies come and meet with the Light.
    Listen hard and put action to the strategies which connect with you.
    Take them. Make them your own. They are yours.

They are Your plan of how to do things.

For those involved, starting with myself, be sure to understand -
    what is the job description
    what are the responsibilities of the job
    what are the goals and objectives
    which ways is the enemy most likely to attack
    what strategy should I rollout.
    how do I implement the plan.

- - -

20 May 2014

Proclamations

Me
Father God, You love me with unconditional love.
I am the apple of Your eye.
You delight in me.
You are proud of me.
You are my Father God and You always back me up in all I do.
You are my everlasting Father.
I will be in health, healed, set right, and walk before the Lord.
I shall declare a thing and it shall come to pass.
I shall decree a thing and it shall be established.
Jesus has made me the head and not the tail.
I am above and not below.
I am valued.
I am appreciated.
I am understood.
And I am loved.
I have all the resources of Your Kingdom, Father God, at my

disposal. They back me up as I live in alignment with You.
I love You Father God.
I delight in the knowledge that I am Your child.
I delight in the knowledge that I live and have my being, because You wanted me.
I delight in knowing that You wanted me to exist and be with You.

Janis
Father God I thank You for Janis' healing.
She will rise from her bed of languishing and *run and not grow weary and walk and not faint.*
She shall delight herself in Your treasurers and Your revelations and declare Your wondrous works throughout the earth.
She shall prosper in everything she sets her hand to.
She shall be *the glory of her husband.*

My Children
They will *grow up like the shoots of the olive.*
They will *fear God and eschew evil.*
They shall *be blessed and prosper.*
They shall find the path to Father's heart and abide in His heart all the days of their lives.
They will be healed, set right, and walk before the Lord.
The curses of generations shall not pass to them or to their seed forever.
They shall *declare a thing and it shall come to pass.*
They shall decree a thing and it shall be established.

My Call
I have everything necessary within my spirit for life and godliness.
No weapon formed against me can prosper.
The creation of God will work together to prosper me in all that

I do.
I am above and not beneath.
I am welcomed into the Throne Room and in the Strategy Room.

Pray for the circumstances of Hitchin
Disperse the cloud of lies that each church is an independent autonomous unit.
Daniel prayed 21 days. No one came to help Gabriel, except Michael.

- - -

22 May 2014

Declarations

Jesus, I declare that You are the Son of God Most High.
Jesus, I declare that You are the Beloved of the Father.
Jesus, I declare that You are the Word of the Father.
Jesus, I declare that You are the Word that created all things.
Jesus, I declare that You are of the same substance and being as the Father.
Jesus, I declare that You are co-equal with the Father and the Spirit.
Jesus, I declare that the Father has exalted You above His name.
Jesus, I declare that the Father has given all things into Your hand.
Jesus, I declare that all power and authority have been given to You.
Jesus, I declare that You are the Lord of lords.
Jesus, I declare that You are the King of kings.
Jesus, I declare that You are the Prince of Peace.
Jesus, I declare that You are the Alpha and Omega, the beginning and the end of all things. You are above all things. And You will judge all things.

Jesus, I declare that all things have their existence in You. And all things have their consummation in You.

Jesus, there is no other god beside You, - You who are one God with the Father and the Spirit.

Jesus, You are God over the United Kingdom.
Jesus, You are God over England.
Jesus, You are King over our queen.
Jesus, You are the Ruler over all government, and their delegated authority is from You.
Jesus, I declare that the government is upon Your shoulders.
Jesus, You are Prince over the Prince of the Power of the Air, who seeks to deceive our country.
Jesus, You are Prince over the Forces of Darkness who seek to derail our corporate God-given destiny.
Jesus, You have conquered and spoiled Satan and his hordes and left them to an open shame.

Jesus, You are Lord over our government in Westminster.
Jesus, You are the Power over and above those who administrate governmental decrees.
Jesus, You are the one and only Saviour of the UK people.
Jesus, there is no other god or saviour but You.
Jesus, You are the Authority that is over and above our County Council.
Jesus, You are Lord over my town of Hitchin.
Jesus, You are God over my house and in my house.
Jesus, You are my Lord and Saviour over my wife and each of my children.
Jesus, I praise You.
Jesus, You are my Lord and my God and my King - the Lord of

my life.
Jesus, through You I honour the Father.
Jesus, You are Lord over my family line. I submit it, past, present and future, into Your hands.
Jesus, You are the eyes that look on me and love me and hold me up.
Jesus, You are the One on whom I must keep my eyes focused.
Jesus, You are the One in whose Light I rest, and in Your Light I see Light.
Jesus, You are the One who made me Light.
Jesus, You are the One who gave me everything pertaining unto life and godliness.
Jesus, You are Lord over my life.
Jesus, You are Lord over my ministry.
Jesus, You are Lord over my church.
Jesus, You are Lord over my God-given destiny.
Jesus, You are my covering and protection.
Jesus, You are the covering and protection over everyone who has placed themselves under my authority.
Jesus, I praise You.
Jesus, You are Lord of my health, You are Lord of my wife's health, and You are Lord of my children's health.
In Your presence we are complete.

- - -

13 June 2014

More declarations

Jesus Christ came to seek and save those who are lost.
Jesus Christ died so we can be restored to relationship with God the Father.

Jesus Christ came to destroy the works of the devil.
Jesus Christ came to reconcile us to the Father.
Jesus Christ came to take back the authority yielded to the devil.
Jesus Christ came to heal the sick.
Jesus Christ came to restore the broken and hurting.
Jesus Christ came to conquer death and the grave.
Jesus Christ came to take away the sin of the world.
Jesus Christ is Lord of lords and King of kings.
Jesus Christ is the Word of the Father, exalted above every name.

All power and authority has been given to Jesus Christ, who is the Word of God, the Only-Begotten Son of God, who is Saviour, Redeemer, Healer, Restorer of the Breach, who is the First Fruit of those who are raised from the dead.

He is Lord. He is God. He is co-equal with the Father and the Spirit, one God, eternal, omnipotent, omnipresent, who created all things and in whom all things subsist.

Jesus Christ is the ultimate expression of God's love towards us. And I love Him.

- - -

18 June 2014

Meaning of Strategy & Tactics

Strategy:
    1. a plan of action designed to achieve a long-term or overall aim.
    2. the art of planning and directing overall military operations and movements in a war or battle.

Tactics:
1. art of disposing armed forces in order of battle and of organising operations, especially during contact with an enemy.

- - -

26 June 2014

Possible strategies of the enemy

1. Prison
Watch for sin openings in habics, which allow for imprisoning.

2. Sleep
Encourage and persuade people that the things of God are boring, so they zone out and go to sleep.

3. Sin
Engineer a sin situation to sever the connection with God.

4. Confusion
Have demons to cause confusion, torment and get the person to blame God.

5. Busyness
Keep people so busy with the affairs of life that they don't stop or allow time for God.

6. Proud loyalty
Encourage pride and loyalty to hinder people changing allegiance.

- - -

27 June 2014

God puts the lonely in families

God puts the lonely in families.

International Centre of Reconciliation.

People are already asking to come.
    They need places to stay.
    They need places to gather.

    Coffee shop.
    Intercessory room.
    Ministry rooms.
    Admin office.
    Corporate worship/Quiet time place.

- - -

27 June 2014

IRC Prayer

- Holy Father, Lord, I pray for the establishing of the International Reconciliation Centre.

- I pray for a team of committed staff and volunteers who will help make this a reality.

- I pray for a venue which can be used as a Gathering Place, which can be used for Corporate Worship or Quiet Time.

- I pray for a Coffee Shop which includes
    a Gospel Shop which can be linked to or which can house

an Intercessory Room, Ministry Rooms, and an Admin Office.

- I also pray for accommodation for those who visit.

- I pray for outside space which visitors can use for Quiet Time, or for Work, or for Sport.

- I pray for Funding.

- I pray for the right people who have the appropriate skills and experience to bring all this into being.

- I pray for security and protection.

- I pray for Your favour and continued direction in this matter.

- - -

29 June 2014

IRC does not get the buildings

IRC does not get the buildings first, or the real estate.
Let the people come and as the numbers grow, set about accommodating them.

- - -

30 June 2014

IRC strategy - 1

- have to be given to hospitality and welcome visitors.

- have to have 'open' times which people can rely on.

- have to have a place to go, e.g. Bancroft or Windmill Hill, to hang out

- must come with a large umbrella .

- - -

3 July 2014

Possible IRC weekly timetable

Sunday
15.00-16.30 - Informal gathering - church meeting

Monday
10.00-10.30 - Morning Prayer
14.00-15.30 - Ministry Time
20.00-21.00 - Ministry Time

Tuesday
10.00-10.30 - Morning Prayer
19.00-21.00 - Andrew Wommack Discipleship Course Training

Wednesday
10.00-10.30 - Morning Prayer

Thursday
10.00-10.30 - Morning Prayer
19.30-22.00 - Healing Deliverance & Restoration Meeting

Friday
10.00-10.30 - Morning Prayer

Saturday
14.00-17.00 - Open House

- - -

22 July 2014

Joshua again

I looked at the Lord, needing refreshing after yesterday's two sessions with SRA survivors. I felt yucky and somewhat defiled. There had been so much junk flying around, I wanted cleansing again.

I had been in the Strategy Room. There was other activity over the Strategy Table.

I understood that the people who come, whom we are to welcome, are the army for taking the town.

(I had been chewing over how the Book of Joshua can be applied to the present day, post Calvary. Clearly I could not go out into the town and put everyone to the sword. The Police would not be happy. So how does this apply to Hitchin.)

Joshua had an army to take the city of Jericho. Where is my army?

The strategy is to follow the Lord's direction.
The strategy for each battle can be different.
The strategy for taking Ai was different to the strategy for taking Jericho. It involved ambush.

The strategy for Hitchin is that the Lord will be bringing people to the town. Their objective is to get free and to connect with Him, and in doing so, they will also take the land at the same time (as a spin-off or side effect).

It will happen and it will be the Lord's doing and be marvellous in our eyes.

23 July 2014

Possible enemy strategy against revival

Enemy strategy
1. send homosexuals to shut down the work using the law.
2. use violence and intimidation.

So, we will welcome all.
- we will welcome homosexuals and have gatherings for them.
- we will welcome bikers and have gatherings for bikers.
- we will welcome ex-cons and have gatherings for them too.

I pray for the ladies who will run the hospitality.

I pray for the prophets and guardians.

I pray for Your angels of protection and for miracles.

- - -

28 July 2014

They belonged before they believed

(Bill Johnson at Harrogate)

Isaiah 60

The disciples belonged before they believed.
Mark 4. Storm. "Who is this guy?"

Value system - people tasted that they belonged.
Sometimes people just need to belong.

The Lord's approach to the Kingdom is very different. Western culture majors on the right of individuals to choose. Jesus didn't.

God shifts focus from local churches to Kingdom. It's not about our ministry. It is about the King!

Isaiah 60:1-2. Your light has come.
John 1. Jesus is the Light.
Joyful anticipation of good - the antidote to 'anti-hope spirit'.

Isaiah 60:3. You are the light. Salt of the earth. Impact (engage) the community.

Jesus' disciples belonged to the community. Didn't view them as a project (or even worse - as the enemy).

Reign means I know how to navigate betrayal, shipwreck - it doesn't take me out.

- - -

30 July 2014

A vision of Hitchin

During one of the times of worship at the Harrogate Pastors' Conference, I saw the pavements of Hitchin coated with Gold. They shimmered with all the colours of the rainbow.

This is from the Strategy Room about Hitchin - more specifically I was shown a stretch of Bancroft.
Bancroft is the nub. It is a centre of spiritual outflow. The enemy has been trying to desecrate it for centuries.

The water flowing over the pavements is gold.

15 August 2014

This flowed off from above the Strategy Table

(This flowed off from above the Strategy Table into me.)

There was a rectangular table and towards one end of it stood a transparent container like a beaker, not glass but something like plastic.

Milk and cream were pouring into the container.

The milk and cream were overflowing the beaker onto the table and covering the table, dripping off the edges.

Even though the container was not in the centre of the table, it was overflowing onto the whole tabletop equally, and dripping off all the edges of the table equally.

- - -

28 August 2014

Stay in the classroom

A classroom is a place to receive instruction.
Always be at that place to receive instruction from the Lord and never go back on it.

In Jeremiah 34, Nebuchadnezzar was fighting against Jerusalem, and the people made a covenant with King Zedekiah to let their slaves go free. They had passed through the two halves of the calf, but later some of the people went back on it and forced their freed slaves back into servitude. Judgement was pronounced against them.

Always be at a place of receiving instruction.

Obeying is like affirming your covenant with the Lord.

Once you understand and have agreed with the instruction, do not go back on it.

Be of one mind.

Be at that place of humility to receive instruction from the Lord and it will go well with you.

- - -

Psalm 25:12-15 (NKJV)
> *Who is the man that fears the Lord?*
> *Him shall He teach in the way He chooses.*
> *He himself shall dwell in prosperity, and his descendants shall inherit the earth.*
> *The secret of the Lord is with those who fear Him, and He will show them His covenant.*
> *My eyes are ever toward the Lord, for He shall pluck my feet out of the net.*

- - -

29 September 2014

I missed a call from Carolina

I missed a call from Carolina and rang her back.

I saw you sitting at a table with other men, but the table was above the earth, and yet the earth was (spinning) over the table.

You were the newest one there.

- - -

10 October 2014

Some more about the Strategy Room

I went to St Mary's Church in the centre of town for some quiet time.

In the Strategy Room the job description and guidelines just rolled off the table into me. I had been turning over in my mind what the role entailed and how I would be brought up to speed from being simply an observer, to being a full participant.

Suddenly I knew that the rollout of the plans are for the colonels to implement, not the generals.

Generals oversee and check that the colonels roll out the plans in a timely fashion, as per their plans.

There is no strife, no pressure in the Strategy Room.
There is no doubt that these might not get implemented.
And yet God honours people by involving us.

So what is the job description and what are the guidelines?

The job description is:
Be there. Be aligned. Be receptive.

The guidelines are:
Be observant.
Bring back to the table such feedback as you gather.

Wow! Simple.

No pressure.
Everything is in hand.
It is just Father's good pleasure to involve people and share His joy of rollout with them.

As I grow in the job, so too will the quality of information that is revealed to me, (that I see,) and so too will the level of my authority and involvement grow.

- - -

14 October 2014

I had a brief time in the Strategy Room

I had a brief time in the Strategy Room today.
On the table was an oblong tray of breads. They looked more like apple turn-overs than breads.
One was missing from the tray. It was spinning in the air above the tray.
The treats were there because it was a celebration of some kind, and someone had brought the tray of breads for the others to enjoy.

I thought/asked, "What can I bring to the table to please everyone, including my Lord?"
Instantly the vision of the marble piazza and the semi-circular house came into my mind playing like a video. I was shocked.
How would that bring pleasure to those at the table?
How would that fit?

It doesn't make sense, - as yet.

- - -

20 October 2014

It was at 4 pm

It was at 4 pm when praise arose from the marble piazza.

- - -

24 October 2014

I give you authority over all the power

Psalm 89:48
Can he deliver his life from the power of the grave?

Jesus said, "I give you authority over all the power of the enemy."

Authority is the right to be in dominion over something else.

If something is acting illegitimately against your legitimate authority, call for the enforcers.

Satan is a conquered foe. The redemption price which Satan engineered, and had to be paid, was paid by Christ. But Satan is continuing to harass God's children, and is acting illegally in many cases, as if the redemption price has not been paid.

Except where God's children step out of harmony with God's Word, the enemy has no right to do or to cause damage.

Where someone has been overwhelmed (conquered), no legal right exists.

Where someone has been conquered, call for the avenger, the deliverer, Isaiah 61:2, and the day of vengeance of our God.

I have authority to say,
"Father, may I call for the day of vengeance of our God, to redress what Satan has done to Janis. May I call for the enforcers to put it right? I use the authority Jesus gave me over all the power of the enemy, and I proclaim today to be the day of the enforcers to deal with Janis' situation, in the name of Jesus. Come enforcers and conquer that which has overwhelmed Janis."

- - -

24 October 2014

May I come into the Strategy Room

May I come into the Strategy Room, Lord? I need to sit and bask in Your Light.

I feel light all down my left side, but not down my right. Is this significant? Why is my left side free to receive, but my right seems not to be able?

Lord, please come with Your extractors and remove any DHSs, curses, demons, whatever, from my right side, so that I might receive from You. I renounce murder, ancestral murder, the worship of animals, and the adoption of animal spirits. I ask for Your forgiveness for down the ages.
Let them be removed now.

Your light is healing the hurts and the sores of my right half of my body, from head to foot. I praise You Lord.

Today is a sitting and waiting day in the Strategy Room. No one knows the day or the hour, not even the Son. Only the Father alone knows.

Lord, let me sit in Your Presence and wait.

The Holy Spirit is on my right hand side. He is my guide and leads me where I should go. Sadly I don't always listen to Him. Just like the vision of the marble piazza and the semi-circular house, the Holy Spirit was on my right hand side as I sat on the arm of the sofa. So too now, Holy Spirit is sitting at my right hand, at the table with me.

I put that vision over the table some days ago.

Maybe the important thing is the place and Presence of the Holy Spirit.

Romans 8:14
> *For as many are lead by the Spirit of God, these are sons of God.*

1 Corinthians 6:17
> *But he that is joined unto the Lord is one spirit with the Lord.*

Ephesians 2:18
> *For through Him we both have access by one Spirit unto the Father.*

- - -

24 October 2014

Check I have the answers

Check I have the answers to the following:

Strategy Room:
  1. What is the job description of my part in the Strategy Room.

2. What are the responsibilities.

3. What are the priorities of the Strategy Room

Knight/General:

4. What is the job description of a Knight/General.

5. What are the responsibilities

How they fit together:

6. How do the priorities of the Strategy Room fit in with the calling and present circumstances.

- - -

31 October 2014

Everyone in the Strategy Room is waiting

In the Strategy Room everyone is waiting to see how far we (and others) have got with the rollouts, so far.

Timing is important. A plan has order and sequence. Certain things must be in place first, before other things can be activated.

Let me check on how we are doing.

- - -

3 November 2014

My part in this

- keep bringing Hitchin before the Lord

- remind Him of His visions and words with thanksgiving

- bring young people involved in drugs and prostitution before the Lord

- pray for the protection of marriages and family units, and the proper nurturing of children

- pray for the businesses and commercial prosperity of Hitchin

- encourage others, reminding them that Hitchin is very much on God's heart

- pray for the correct discipling of young people, and always to have the freedom and ability to share Jesus with others

- pray for the protection of families to have time together for prayer

- ask the Lord to raise up and bring in spiritual mums and dads, leaders, teachers and preachers, who can equip others to live in deep relationship with the Lord

- ask the Lord to put in place the necessary infrastructure and favour with the local businesses and the local council

- study the book of Joshua. Learn how the Lord lead Joshua in taking the land

- thank the Lord for giving authority over the land

- enquire about what authority over the land entails, and what are the responsibilities which come with the privilege

- wait on the Lord to hear direction about how to take the land, spiritually

- move in Kingdom authority

- Thank the Lord for the privilege of being part of His end-time plan

- worship God

- use worship to dig a well or a portal. Worship maintains an open heaven

- practise the Presence of God and take Him everywhere you go and involve Him in everything you do. Listen all the time to Him

- do not presume that the directions from the Lord will be the same every time or will be what you think they should be

- pray for the establishing of the International Reconciliation Centre

- ask the Lord to assemble the team of committed staff and volunteers to run it

- ask the Lord for a Coffee Shop and a Gospel Shop and an Intercessory Room and a Quiet Worship Room and for Ministry Rooms and an Admin Office

- ask the Lord to open up accommodation for those who visit

- ask the Lord for outside space visitors can use for Quiet Time, Work, and Sport

- ask the Lord to send the funding as it is needed

- ask the Lord to bring together the right people who have the necessary skills and experience to make the International Reconciliation Centre a reality - to bring it into being

- pray for security and protection of the people involved, their families and loved ones

- pray for the security and protection of the vision, the rollout and the Anointing and Presence

- ask the Lord to put His favour on this endeavour, and to give us direction continually, so we don't go awry

- pray that we remain given to hospitality

- pray that we remain consistent and constant in our 'opening times'

- ask the Lord to destroy the plans and purposes of the enemy in respect of Hitchin and the International Reconciliation Centre

- ask the Lord to send us people given to hospitality, prophets and watchmen, guardians, angels of protection, and angels carrying miracles

- be willing, available and determined to walk our personal paths, with our steps washed with butter - walk the Word

- be ready to receive and correctly steward the rivers of oil - the Anointing

- be available and willing to allow the Presence and Anointing to overflow onto others

- be willing to receive instruction and be told, especially by the Lord. Put yourself at the place of receiving instruction

- be of one mind

- keep yourself at the footstool of the Throne of Grace

- - -

14 November 2014

Authority over the land entails

Lord, what does authority over the land entail?
What is the job description?
What are the responsibilities?

(I understand that a job description enables a person to perform whatever role they have been given, and understanding the responsibilities of the job helps a person to measure how well they are doing in their stewardship.)

Lord, You dropped into my spirit the Scripture that those who have entered into Your rest have ceased from their own work. How does all this fit together?
As a bride is brought to the bridegroom, so too does the Lord bring the building of a work to those whose place it is to run it. Let the Lord build the house. Cease from your own solutions and simply call into being that which the Lord shows, should be built. The servants of the Lord will build the house for you. You maintain your place of rest in the Lord. Everything about the Lord is Grace. He is love. He is provision.

Once the house has been built, go in and occupy it. Possess it. Dwell in it. It gives the Lord great pleasure to do this for you. (Cease from your own work and remain - abide - in His rest.)

Your time with Me will allow Me to share My heart for what I wish to build in your life.
Use faith. See it. Believe that the Lord is, and is a rewarder of those who diligently seek Him.

Stay connected and use your faith to believe that the Lord desires to do this for you. Call it into being. Call it as if it were. And it will come into being - a work of the Lord - and it will be marvellous in your eyes.

Authority over the land has been brought to you (like the bride is brought). It is yours. Possess it. It has been given to you. Abide in it. Walk in it. But do not use it to create an Ishmael.
Use the authority over the land to call into being the things God wants established in the land.
The act of you hearing My heart and calling it as if it were, is the act of permission I require in order to build in that part of creation over which I gave you dominion.
Dominion and authority are not the same.
When your faith is in alignment with My desire for you, then something is born. It comes into being.

So the job description of having authority over the land is about listening to the beat of My heart - receiving revelation about what I wish to establish in the area over which I have given you authority.
I gave you this authority because I wish to partner with you in the bringing of the Kingdom to earth.

Therefore in order to measure how well you fulfil your role, log all My heart's downloads to you. Receive them as your own dreams. Accept them. Dwell in them. Live in them and let them live in you. Talk about them. Watch them come into being and tick them off your list. This is the Lord's doing and it is marvellous in your eyes.

The responsibilities are - that if you do not align yourself with My will, My Kingdom cannot be established through you, and I will not be able to honour you or reward you in the way I would like to.

I will search for another who will walk in harmony with Me. But God does not make mistakes. I have chosen the right person in you, because your heart is right before Me.

- - -

27 November 2014

Cafe Nero and seeing the seven Rs of the IRC

I am in Cafe Nero reading through my journal. I keep getting the picture of a wall in the reception area of a modern building in the IRC and there is lettering on the wall - words which are 3D set out from the wall. I think they are the seven Rs.

I am also sensing in my back that this is real and will come to pass in the future, because the vision has been released from heaven.

- - -

28 November 2014

To Do - From previous journal entries

- The Strategy Room in heaven should be copied on earth so we stay in tune with what is decided in heaven.

- Make a habit of using Proclamations, Declarations and Decrees to bring into being what comes out of the Strategy Room.

- Pray for the circumstances of the town.

- The Protocol in heaven's Strategy Room is:
    ~ Sit in the Light. Be a light.
    ~ Listen. Be aligned.
    ~ Be receptive. Put into action what is received.
    ~ Make it your own. Accept responsibility for bringing it into the physical realm.
    ~ Give feedback on the current circumstances and how the rollout is going.

- He will bring the young people first, then the older ones, and then the children.
    ~ young people students
    ~ young people unemployed
    ~ young people single parents
    ~ young people carers
    ~ those trapped in drugs
    ~ those trapped in prostitution

- Visions:
    ~ groups of 2,3,4 young people sharing the gospel with shoppers in Bancroft
    ~ spontaneous gatherings in the parks
    ~ family and friends home prayer groups
    ~ field of young people connecting with God
    ~ established churches helping and enabling these events
    ~ schools making their accommodation available
    ~ homes responding with hospitality

- To take the town:
    ~ conquer the spiritual structure
    ~ use the authority of Jesus (doing everything in His name)
    ~ overcome the spiritual atmosphere

~ walk in Kingdom authority in all we do
~ keep in alignment with the Light and carry the Presence with you.
~ do not be concerned about people's freedom to hold other opinions or beliefs - respect their right to this freedom
~ show the faith you hold in your heart by outworkings of love
~ give permission for God's angels to do their part
~ where there is darkness, be light (Isaiah 60)
~ the book of Joshua shows that the Lord had a different strategy for each battle - maintain alignment with the Lord and constantly involve Him and follow His direction
~ we have been given the authority to take our town (see Acts)

- Jesus has already laid waste all principalities and powers. Don't listen to the lies and propaganda of the enemy.

- Jesus has already given us authority over all the power of the enemy. Remember, an ambassador does not do the fighting, the spiritual troops do the fighting.

- Dig a well (portal) with worship. Maintain it with worship.

- Deal with territorial and water spirits. Deal with the curses.

- Carry the Presence of God as clothing (robes) of your ambassadorship.

- The people we welcome to the town, to visit or to stay, are the army who will take the town. This will be a byproduct of them getting free and connecting with God.

- - -

9 December 2014

Prince of the power of the air Ephesians 2:2

Parallel Verses of Ephesians 2:2

Young's Literal Translation
in which once ye did walk according to the age of this world, according to the ruler of the authority of the air, of the spirit that is now working in the sons of disobedience

King James Bible
Wherein in time past ye walked according to the course of this world, according to the prince [archon - a *first* (in rank or power): - chief prince, ruler] of the power [exousia - **authority, jurisdiction**, power, right, strength] of the air, [aer - air (as naturally *circumambient*): - air] the spirit that now worketh in the children of disobedience:

New International Version
in which you used to live when you followed the ways of this world and of the ruler of the kingdom of the air, the spirit who is now at work in those who are disobedient.

New Living Translation
You used to live in sin, just like the rest of the world, obeying the devil - the commander of the powers in the unseen world. He is the spirit at work in the hearts of those who refuse to obey God.

- - -

19 December 2014

In the Strategy Room

Welcome back.
Thank You Lord.

What type of feedback do You want?
What you see, your perceptions, your feelings.

There's a lot going on in my personal life - and a concern that I am so time limited that I feel I cannot give the wider issues of Church, country, or international arena, the intercessory time I feel they should have.
I suspect a smoke screen of the enemy, thinking that trapping me in busyness is delaying Your plans. But I know You have already foreseen that.
I have feelings about the wider issues, but can only really focus on our personal issues at the moment, since Janis is requiring so much time and attention. Yet I know that the love, care and time planted into Janis will yield harvests.

On the wider issues, I am grieved about my own country, England, and the government ministers passing laws which call wrong right, calling perversity normal. The latest directives are against all who hold Your Word in their hearts. And now it is illegal to disagree with the government on the laws it has passed - even though they are without a mandate from the people, and inspite of the massive protest of the largest petition ever, representing more than half a million people, which was ignored and which by law should have forced the matter back into Parliament to be re-discussed. But they refused to do it, putting themselves above the law. Now laws are being imposed. The fruit of the tree is not good.

On the international scene, I sense the rollout of the enemy's plans to squeeze You out of people's consciousness. People in many lands have seemed to have lost their fear of God. Thank God for the Africans who are generally less tolerant of compromise and more militant for the truth.

Yet I see the end-time prophecies in Scripture, and start to feel a bit like Jeremiah during the siege and fall of Jerusalem.

Thy Kingdom come. Thy will be done on earth as it is in heaven.

Injustice gives rise to anger. Anger promotes resentment, and resentment leads to defilement and to violence. Violence breeds fear, and where there is strife, there is all manner of evil.

And yet Jesus, You say not to resist evil and to overcome evil with good.

But what about time?

What about the living that has to be done in between events?

It is an uncomfortable place to be and it is heartbreaking.

What about your personal front?

Lord, You know well the crying and praying Janis has done - the discomfort she is in with her body, and the frustration she experiences because the body does not now do what she would like it to do. We wait for her healing to be manifested - and I thank You for her healing.

I have stopped Sunday meetings and Thursday IHADs.

I recently reviewed my journal and saw Your Word to me last February. You said that the ministry was going to die - let the next generation take it over - and there would be a winter and springtime and summer. You also said that Janis would come to a time of transition. Is this that she will be healed?

I also see that anger and the wrestling with people emotionally is a curse which has come down the generations. I was told it was in the parents, and it is trying to pass onto the children. There is a spirit of anger there, and contention.

I have been finding it tough going. I have sensed stress slowly stealthily building up in me. Please remove it Lord. I don't want it. Let me sit in the Light.

You have done well.
I don't feel like it, Lord.

*I need people in difficult situations as well as people in nice circumstances. Your interaction with Me - Your involving Me - gives Me the permission to be active in the world without violating (*the law of*) free choice.*
Come Lord. Be fully involved, each and every day.

Father's plans are still rolling out. He is the King of Glory. Just as Abram could not be given the land flowing with milk and honey, because the iniquity of the Amorites was not yet full, know also that the end-time plan waits until the sin is full.

Last night Lord, Janis had the TV on and I glimpsed men kissing, two women lustfully looking at each other, and a scene of a naked man and woman having sex at a table top - stuff which a short while ago would have been considered pornographic, but which is now being shown openly in people's living rooms.
I had expected that Sodom and Gomorrah to come about in the streets, but not overtly put on the TV and being pumped into people's living rooms. They don't need to go onto the street. It is

there in front of them. And also what is shown on TV will be emulated in everyday life.

I heard about a couple fornicating openly on the floor of the gents' loo in a night club, while others came in and out to the toilet.

Lawlessness is abounding - from the government to the ordinary person. They have lost their fear of God. They no longer have or want the knowledge of God.

My Word says that I have given them over to a reprobate mind, doing those things which are not seemly or fitting - men with men and women with women.

(Romans 1:26-28)

Lord, I pray for my wife and family, for my team, my town of Hitchin, and my country. I am already an outlaw because of my relationship with You and my respect for Your Word.

Where do we go from here?

Let not your heart be troubled.

You believe in God, believe also in Me.

I told you back in 2006 to keep your eyes on Me and not to be worried about how things will work out.

I am still on the Throne.

My Father has given Me everything. And you and I must maintain our unity.

You do not have to put anything right. That is not your job.

You are a lighted lamp. Your job is to shine in the darkness. And the darkness cannot overcome light. I didn't make it that way. It can't be what it is not, just as you can't be anything other than what you are.

I am pleased with you.

I am proud that you come to Me.

Remain in My love. Dwell in it. Abide in it.

It is Father's good pleasure to give you the Kingdom.

- - -

www.ingramcontent.com/pod-product-compliance
Lightning Source LLC
Chambersburg PA
CBHW071329040426
42444CB00009B/2114